Minja	Bishop
Robin	Hunter

ISRAEL

ISRAEL

by Nora Kubie

illustrated with photographs

REVISED EDITION

FRANKLIN WATTS, INC.
575 Lexington Avenue, New York, N.Y. 10022

This book is dedicated to my fellow members of Ein Hod. And to the old-new state of Israel: may it succeed in all it hopes for its people and as a member of the family of nations.

My thanks are due, for much information, to the Government Press Office, State of Israel; to Miss Malka Ben-Yosef of the Israel Consulate General, New York City, for advice and suggestions; and to the MacDowell Colony of Peterborough, New Hampshire, where I completed the manuscript.
Unless otherwise specified, photographs are courtesy of the Israel Press and Information Office, Tel Aviv and New York.

Library of Congress Catalog Card Number: 68-10611
Printed in the United States of America

2 3 4 5 6

CONTENTS

ISRAEL

Israel in the World

AN EASTERN LAND THAT FACES WEST

Four thousand years ago the patriarch Abraham journeyed with his family and his flocks and herds to the land of Canaan, which his Lord had promised to him and his descendants. "And Abraham dwelt in Beersheba," the Bible tells us.

Beersheba was an oasis in the desert then. Today it is a big bustling city which you can find on a map. It is in Israel, the land that once was Canaan. Israel stands at the crossroads of three continents: Asia, Europe, and Africa. Geographically it is in the part of Asia known as the Middle East, a portion of the Asian continent that is closely related through its history and ideas with Europe and the Americas.

Ancient Israel gave us the Bible, the source of Western religion. It is the land of King David and King Solomon and the Hebrew prophets; the land where Jesus was born and died; a holy land for both Jews and Christians. Yet it was always a small country, and it still is.

Israel is also, to most of us, a faraway land, although modern means of transportation have made the world seem smaller. In the days of sailing ships, it was half a world away from the New World. Today a plane can travel from New York to Israel between sunrise and sunset of a summer day — and flying time is constantly growing shorter. An amazing number of people visit Israel each year. Some want to see the places mentioned in the Bible, and others to find out how the state of Israel, born in 1948, is getting along.

JET'S-EYE VIEW

If you were to go to Israel by air, you might fly in a jet of Israel's national airline, El Al, a name which means "skyward." If you could fly high enough and had eyes sharp enough, you would see the whole country rolled out below like a map.

From high above, you would see the railroad that connects the big cities of Haifa, Tel Aviv, Jerusalem, and Beersheba, and then continues to crawl southward. You would see a network of roads being widened and extended. You would see the river Jordan, looking like a string with three blue beads upon it. The tiny northern bead is all that is left of a one-time marshy lake, recently drained to make the fertile Hula Valley. From here the Jordan flows down to the large lake known as the Sea of Galilee (also called Lake Kinneret, or Lake Tiberias). Then it twists and winds and wriggles southward to empty into the Dead Sea, the lowest spot on earth. Though landlocked, the sea is so salty that no fish live in it. You might be surprised at how many different patterns and colors and kinds of landscape there are in this little country.

In the north is Galilee: green valleys and tree-covered mountains; old towns and Arab villages looking as if they had been piled in a heap on the hillsides; and farm settlements spread out over the valleys.

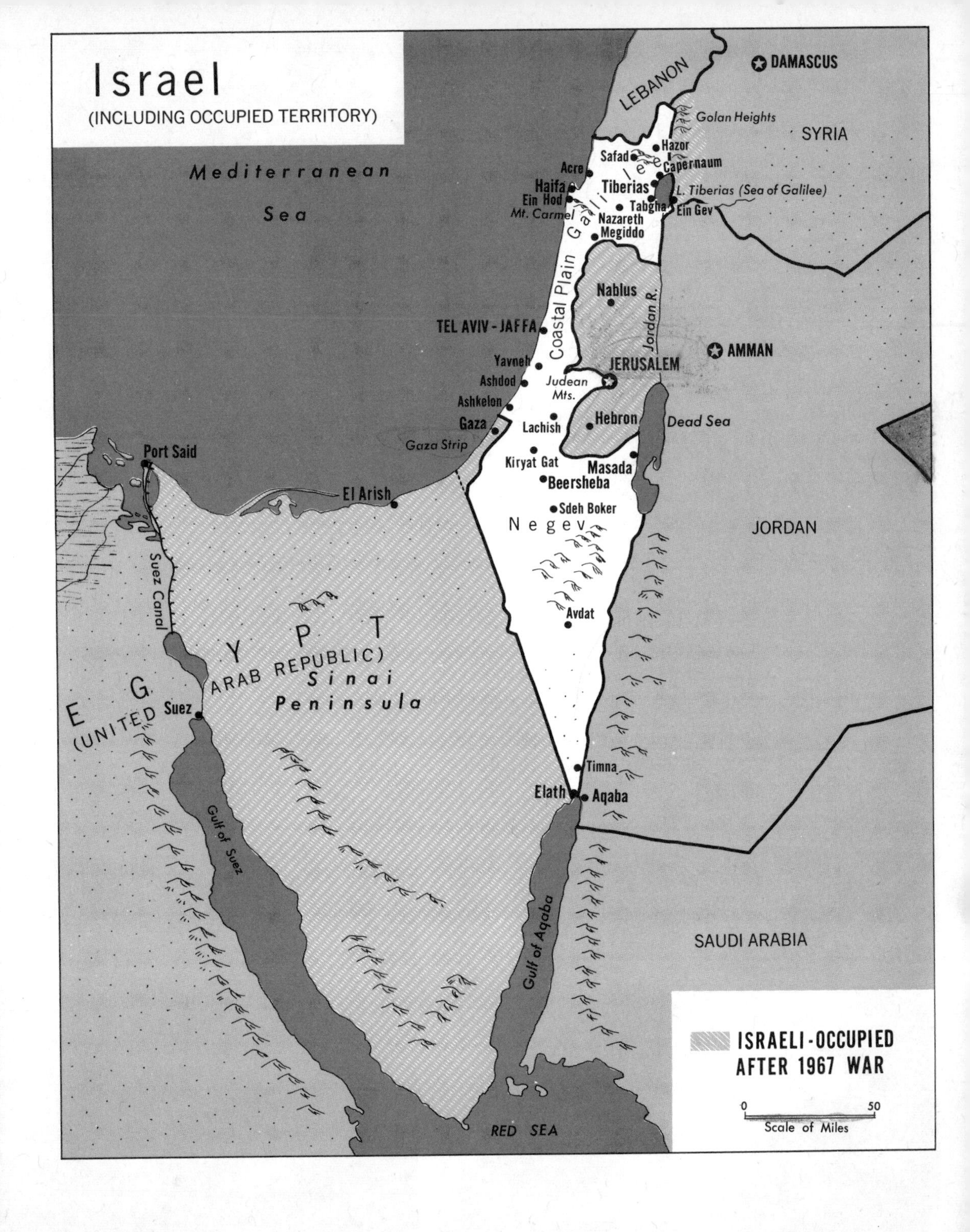

Israel
(INCLUDING OCCUPIED TERRITORY)
Mediterranean
Sea
LEBANON
DAMASCUS
Golan Heights
SYRIA
Hazor
Safad
Capernaum
Acre
Haifa
Tiberias
L. Tiberias (Sea of Galilee)
Ein Hod
Tabgha
Ein Gev
Mt. Carmel
Nazareth
Galilee
Megiddo
Coastal Plain
Nablus
Jordan R.
TEL AVIV-JAFFA
AMMAN
Yavneh
JERUSALEM
Ashdod
Judean Mts.
Ashkelon
Gaza
Lachish
Hebron
Dead Sea
Gaza Strip
Port Said
Kiryat Gat
Masada
Beersheba
El Arish
Sdeh Boker
Negev
JORDAN
Suez Canal
Avdat
EGYPT
(UNITED ARAB REPUBLIC)
Sinai
Peninsula
Suez
Timna
Elath
Aqaba
Gulf of Suez
Gulf of Aqaba
SAUDI ARABIA
ISRAELI-OCCUPIED
AFTER 1967 WAR
0
50
Scale of Miles
RED SEA

Above, left: Fertile farmland of the Hula Valley in the north. Above, right: Ben Yehuda Street in Jerusalem. Below, left: Palm trees line a Tel Aviv street. Below, right: The Wilderness of Zin, in the Negev, where Moses wandered with the Children of Israel.

In the center is the coastal plain that runs along the Mediterranean, bordered along most of its 117 miles with yellow sands. This is a region of fields, fruit groves, villages, and towns, including sprawling Tel Aviv, Israel's largest city. Inland from the coastal plain, between north and south, are the ridged and stony Judean mountains, and Jerusalem, the capital of Israel.

In the south is the Negev triangle, which begins at Beersheba, and ends in a point at Elath, on the Gulf of Aqaba. Once all of the Negev was wilderness. Most of it still is. Here and there in the brown barrens, you will see a tuft of green marking a settlement, or blocks of houses and checkerboards of streets: new cities in the desert.

THE BIBLE AS HISTORY

A citizen of the modern state of Israel is an *Israeli.* The ancestors of the Jews were called *Israelites,* or *Hebrews.* The large majority of Israelis are Jews, although not too many practice the religion of Judaism in the strictly orthodox fashion. But almost every Israeli child knows the Old Testament, for it is the history of his country and of his ancestors. Archeologists — the scholars who dig up the places where ancient people lived — have proved the accuracy of much Bible history that was once thought to be legend.

It was Abraham's grandson Jacob who gave the name to the land and the people. Jacob wrestled one night with a messenger of the Lord, and when morning came, was told that his name would no longer be Jacob but Israel — one who demands justice from God. Jacob's descendants therefore are called the Children of Israel.

A print from an eighteenth-century Bible depicts God showing Moses the Land of Promise. (New York Public Library Picture Collection)

During a famine in Canaan, Jacob's sons migrated to Egypt. After several generations, the Children of Israel, greatly increased in numbers, were enslaved. Moses brought them up out of Egypt and back to the land which God had promised them. On their way through the desert, at Mount Sinai, God gave Moses the Law, embodied in the Ten Commandments and a collection of rules for daily life. These rules were later explained by teachers and wise men in a great book called the Talmud.

From these same laws and rules come the ideas of human brotherhood, justice, and peace, upon which the modern state of Israel is founded.

ANCIENT ISRAEL BECOMES A ROMAN PROVINCE

After the Israelites had governed themselves for a while through tribal "judges," they united into one kingdom ruled first by Saul, and later by David and Solomon. This united kingdom defeated its enemy neighbors, enlarged its borders, and achieved prosperity and a brief period of peace. When King Solomon died, about 930 B.C., the country was split into the northern kingdom of Israel, and the southern kingdom of Judah. After some two hundred years the northern kingdom fell to the Assyrians. The fate of its people, the Ten Lost Tribes, is unknown. Some were sent into exile; others probably intermarried with non-Israelites, and forgot their heritage. In 586 B.C., the kingdom of Judah was defeated by Nebuchadnezzar of Babylon. The Temple built by Solomon was destroyed, Jerusalem turned into ashes, and most of its people were carried off to the land of their conqueror. During captivity, the exiles of Judah became known as the Jews.

After about fifty years, the Jews were allowed to return to Jerusalem and rebuild their Temple. This Second Commonwealth enjoyed a measure of self-government for five hundred years, sometimes as part of a larger empire, sometimes under its own kings, the Maccabees and the house of Herod. During this period, the Old Testament was compiled.

Then rose the power of Rome. Germany, Gaul, and Britain were subdued and extended the Roman empire across a good part of the known world. Rome assumed control of Herod's kingdom also and called it Judea. As a Roman province, Judea was in a state of turbulence and difficulty. Crucifixion was a common form of punishment. Among the Jews crucified was Jesus of Nazareth. Seventy years after his birth, the Roman legions put down a Jewish revolt and destroyed the Second Temple.

A model of the Second Temple in Jerusalem.

DIGGING UP A LAST STAND

The bleak rock of Masada rises out of the desert thirteen hundred feet above the Dead Sea. Until a few years ago, it was the ambition of every Israeli child to be able to say that he or she had climbed to its summit. Those who reached it had good reason to be proud. The only way up was the Snake Path on the eastern face of the rock, a climb that was narrow, steep, and slippery with sliding stones.

Masada has been tamed. The Snake Path has been widened and smoothed. Now you can even drive to the foot of the western precipice and stroll comfortably up the path laid on a Roman ramp leading to the summit. The path was made for the workers who excavated the ruins of Masada in 1963 and 1964.

Herod the Great built fortifications, walls, storehouses, and palaces on the summit of Masada, and gouged huge cisterns out of its sides. Except for the winter rains, this is a waterless region, but the king had to have his Roman baths and swimming pool. He selected this rugged rock in the desert as a refuge from his many enemies. One of them was Queen Cleopatra of Egypt, who wanted her Roman admirer Antony to give her Herod's kingdom of Judea. On Herod's death in 4 B.C., Roman legions garrisoned Masada.

It was captured by the Jews at the beginning of the revolt in A.D. 66. When Jerusalem fell four years later, a group of stubborn rebels, the Zealots, held out at Masada for three more years. Below the rock, not far from the camp of modern excavators, are the remains of the camps of the Roman Tenth Legion which besieged the city. The Romans built a ramp of logs and earth to the summit, rolled up siege towers, lobbed stone cannonballs over Masada's

Masada and tents of the volunteers who excavated the ruins.

walls with their catapults, and flung in firebrands. When the wall was breached and there was no hope of holding Masada for more than a few hours, Eleazar, leader of the defenders, addressed his people in a fiery speech. It was better to die, he said, than to be carried off into slavery by the Roman victors. Let ten of the Jewish garrison be chosen by lot to kill the rest, with their wives and children, and then each other, he urged. The last man alive would kill himself.

When the Romans entered the burning fortress in the morning, they found the bodies of nine hundred and sixty men, women, and children. Two women and five children, who had crept off and hidden themselves in underground caverns, lived to tell the tale.

JEWISH SAGES OF GALILEE

The defenders of Masada chose to die rather than to suffer the fate of the remainder of the Jewish population. Many Jews were carried off into captivity after Jerusalem fell. Still others remained. Through the centuries that followed, some returned as pilgrims, or to spend their old age in the sacred land. Now that the Temple and its priests were no more, synagogues became the places to meet, pray, and study. Instead of priests, the rabbis (teachers) became the religious leaders.

Tiberias, a city on the Sea of Galilee, was founded by Herod's son, Herod Antipas, and named for the Roman emperor Tiberius. In its early years, the Jews considered it a wicked pagan city, and the more religious refused to set foot in it. After the fall of the Temple, many learned Jews settled in Tiberias. Here they completed the Jerusalem Talmud, a commentary on Jewish law. Here the famous Spanish-born Jewish medieval doctor and philosopher Maimonides is buried.

The ancient walls of Tiberias on the Sea of Galilee.

Most recent arrivals to this part of the land now occupy the little old houses of black stone, and the ruins half-tumbled into the water, as well as the new housing developments on the steep slopes above the town. Women in the bright flowing robes of Tunis or the pants of Kurdistan mill around the open booths in the market, where oriental spices, plastic dishes, buttons and beads, kerosene stoves, vegetables, fruit, and fish are sold.

The hotels, both in lower Tiberias and in the resort suburb above it, are filled with vacationers, especially in winter when, because it is below sea level, Tiberias is pleasantly warm. These visitors swim in the lake, water-ski, or visit the elegant new health establishment next to the ruins of an ancient Roman bathhouse. Or they ride across the lake in a motorboat to the Israeli settlement of Ein Gev for a fish dinner, or a concert in its fine recital hall. Looking down upon Ein Gev are the cliffs where the gun emplacements of hostile Syria were planted for nineteen years.

In the mountains above Tiberias is Safad, cool in summer when Tiberias is unbearably hot, and cold in winter when Tiberias is warm. Safad, now a summer resort and an artists' colony, has been a holy city since the fifteenth century. Refugees from Spain came there then and established a center for cabalists. These were Jewish wise men who were thought to understand the language of birds and beasts, to speak with angels, and to be able to foretell the future. People in Safad still believe in magic and miracles.

Arabs shop in the market at Nazareth.

NEW TESTAMENT COUNTRY

Galilee is also the setting for stories in the Gospels, the first four books of the New Testament, which relate the life of Jesus. At Capernaum on the north shore of the lake are the ruins of a third-century synagogue, built on the foundation of an earlier one where Jesus preached. It was at Capernaum that Jesus found his first disciples, Simon Peter, Andrew, James, and John, "casting their nets into the sea: for they were fishermen." The Sea of Galilee still teems with fish, which are caught today in the nylon nets of fishermen in gasoline-powered boats.

At Tabgha on the lake shore, a guardian priest will show you an ancient mosaic floor commemorating the Multiplication of the Loaves and Fishes. Nearby is the little hill from which Jesus delivered his Sermon on the Mount; and Magdala, the birthplace of Mary Magdalene, his devoted follower. Cana, now an Arab village, is where Jesus performed his first miracle — turning water into wine at a wedding. It is on the road to Nazareth, the chief goal of Christian pilgrims to Israel.

The old holy city of Safed is now a popular resort town.

Arab women fetch water at Mary's Well in Nazareth.

Nazareth has the largest Arab population in the country. Most of them were converted to Christianity years ago by the fathers who are custodians of the monasteries and churches. A large and elaborate new Church of the Annunciation encloses the underground grotto in which Mary, mother of Jesus, is said to have lived with her parents. And in the main square of Nazareth, Arab women fill their jugs at a drinking fountain known as Mary's Well.

The Jewish newcomers of the last ten years live in tall concrete buildings on the rim of the valley. Many factories have been built nearby. Some Arabs find work as guides to the holy places, and many others as carpenters. One of Nazareth's latest developments is a cooperative carpenter shop. Another cooperative, set up by an American garment manufacturer, employs at its sewing machines Arab girls who a few years ago would not have been allowed out of their homes unchaperoned.

Ruins of a Crusaders' castle at Atlit.

THE DARKEST TIME

The collapse of a final revolt against Rome in the second century, ended the chance of an independent Jewish state for almost two thousand years. The Romans renamed the land Syria Palaestina. And as Palestine it was known till the birth of the state of Israel in 1948.

Because Palestine was a land bridge between the empires of east and west, it knew few years of peace. Beginning with the Arab conquest of the seventh century, wave after wave of the warlike followers of Muhammad occupied it. For only two centuries (1099–1291) was it ruled by European Christians. Crusaders, urged by the popes to rescue the holy places from Muslim hands, mounted a bloody invasion which succeeded for a time in establishing the Latin Kingdom of Jerusalem. The remains of great Crusader castles are scattered about the land. When Acre, the last Christian stronghold, fell and the last of the Knights Templars sailed away, the country was left scorched and desolate. The trees had been chopped down for firewood; goats nibbled what was left of the grass. Winter rains washed away the soil; running streams silted up and spread out into swamps. Ottoman Turks completed the ruin of the Land of Milk and Honey.

Drawings of the stoning and burning of Jews during medieval times. (New York Public Library Picture Collection)

THE RETURN TO ZION

Except for the handful remaining in Palestine, Jews lived in what they called the *Diaspora* — the dispersal, or scattering — all over the world. Wherever permitted to do so, they became loyal citizens of their adopted country.

In many countries, Jews were badly treated. They lived in a ghetto, a separate part of town, sometimes surrounded by a wall.

In Spain in the fifteenth century, Christian officials tortured Jews to make them give up their religion. The Jews were finally expelled from Spain in 1492. In the nineteenth century, Russian Cossacks rode through Jewish villages to beat and murder men, women, and children.

Why did such things happen? Some say it was because Jews were different from the people around them. They refused to become Christians or Muslims. They insisted, in their private lives, on behaving in accordance with the old law of Scripture and the Talmud. Mysterious stories, quite untrue, grew up about their form of worship. Jews who were less religious, or less strict, faced equally harsh treatment, just because they were known to be Jews. It was easy to be cruel to a weak and scattered people.

After each attack, a number of Jews managed to escape to other lands; some to America. The Zionists were those who longed to return to Palestine. They spoke of it as *Zion,* because David, greatest of ancient Israel's kings, built his fortress at Jerusalem on Mount Zion. Religious Zionists believed that the Jews would return to Zion in accordance with the promises of Scripture. Theodor Herzl, an Austrian journalist, saw the return in a different way. The only answer to these anti-Jewish feelings, Herzl thought, was for the Jews to have a land of their own. He wrote of it in his book *Alt-Neüland* (Old New-land), and devoted his life to promoting the idea. He is buried in the national cemetery on Mount Herzl at Jerusalem, capital of the state he foretold but never saw.

At the end of the nineteenth century and the beginning of the twentieth, a good many Jews were migrating to Palestine, not to die of old age and be buried in the sacred soil, but to resettle and rehabilitate the land. They determined to establish in Zion a new idealistic society where all men could live together in peace.

A kibbutz in northern Israel.

THE COLLECTIVE SETTLEMENTS

The first Jewish pioneers in Palestine believed that the Jews had to learn to work the soil with their own hands as they had done before the Diaspora. Unfortunately these were city people with no knowledge of farming. The soil was poor; the climate hard. The settlers would have starved had it not been for help from abroad. Then a group of young people discovered a way to survive by helping one another. In 1909, Degania, the first of the collective settlements, was founded.

The land they had bought was considered by its Arab owners to be useless, unhealthy swamp. Its largest crop was the deadly malarial mosquito. The pioneers lived in tents, without heat, electric light, inside plumbing, or other conveniences. After they had dug trenches to drain the swamp water, cleared the ground, and planted trees and crops, their farm began slowly to produce.

Others followed the example of Degania. It was a hard life at first. Even when the settlers moved from tents into shacks, they lacked most of the comforts we take for granted. Before the swamps were completely dry, many settlers died of the malaria which had killed Arab peasants before them. There was so much work to be done that women had to work in the fields alongside the men instead of spending all their time at home looking after their husbands and children. Besides, the young women believed that they should have the same rights and the same tasks as men. Both men and women were socialists who claimed that no person should own private property or pay others to work for them.

Today there are more than two hundred *kibbutzim* (collective settlements) in Israel. Although differing in the strictness of their rules, and in some of their ideas, they are all organized in much the same way. Everything — property, buildings, machinery, animals — is owned jointly by a group numbering anywhere from sixty members to two thousand. A candidate for membership can be accepted or rejected after a trial period of living in the kibbutz. A child is born into membership.

Children on a kibbutz do not live with their parents, but in a house with other children the same age. An older member supervises the house, but does not live there. The chairs and tables, the wash basins and showers, and the hooks for toothbrushes and clothing are all at the right height for children, so that they learn to look after themselves when they are very young.

Kindergarten and primary school classes are held in the children's houses. When a child is old enough he attends a neighborhood high school shared by boys and girls of several settlements. Exceptionally gifted youngsters and those with special talents are sometimes sent outside the kibbutz to college or technical school, or abroad for graduate training.

Even very young children have jobs to do in addition to their lessons. They help to set the tables for meals in their house, and

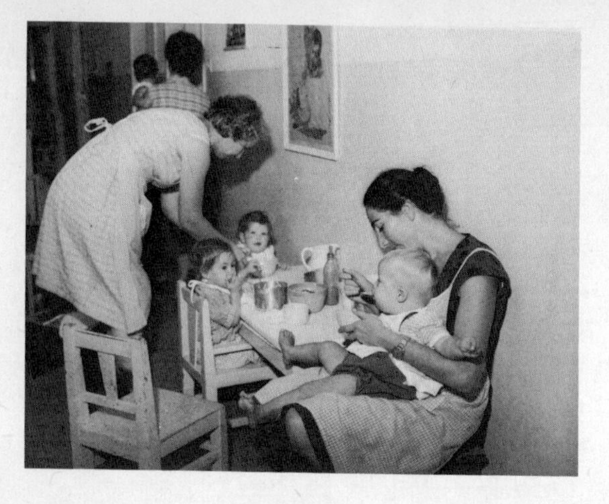

Feeding time at a babies' house on a kibbutz.

feed the animals in the children's farm nearby. There is, however, time for play as well as for work. In summer there is a daily visit to a beach or swimming pool. There are games on the lawn. On holidays the youngsters take part in a play or a parade.

Adults work very hard, but in the late afternoon, when their jobs are done for the day, parents take their children to their own homes. The parents' home is a room, or at most a room and a half. It is well furnished, usually with books, pictures, a radio, a teakettle, and a few other personal things. No kitchen equipment other than the kettle is necessary because all the adults in a settlement eat in a common dining hall. The food is cooked and served by the members, men as well as women.

At bedtime the children return to their own house. They are not alone then either, for each child shares a room with two or three other children. Roommates are like brothers or sisters to one another.

On Friday nights there are white cloths and flowers on the tables in the dining halls, where the children and their parents have dinner together. They also spend all day Saturday together. On weekdays a child might visit his parents at work, because it is probably nearby.

An elected committee runs the kibbutz and decides what sort of work everyone is best fitted for. Women no longer do heavy farm work. Today a woman may be a teacher, or a nurse in the babies' house; she may work in the laundry, or in the sewing room. A man may work in the cow barns, or in a factory which both supplements the income from the farm and gives work to elderly members. Even though they may do different kinds of work, men and women are regarded as equals.

By now many of the collectives have become prosperous and comfortable. They include on their premises a swimming pool, a culture house for concerts, movies, and visiting theatrical companies; and a dining hall with picture windows and shiny up-to-date equipment.

But new collective settlements are still being founded by young pioneers in remote spots where living is difficult, on borders where it is dangerous. Without such people, Israel would not have survived in peace or war. Many of the most important government officials, members of the congress and the cabinet, were (and still are) *kibbutzniks*.

Not all farms in Israel are collectives. There are also cooperative villages where each family has its own house and land to do with as it pleases. The members of a cooperative join together to buy the heavy machinery and seeds that they need, to sell their produce, and to pay the salaries of doctors, nurses, teachers, and managers of the cooperative store.

And of course, there are villages where nothing is owned jointly. Because the early Zionists believed so earnestly in the value of tilling the soil, and because the land must be restored before Israel can feed itself, there is so much talk about the agricultural way of life that a visitor is apt to think that this is a nation of farmers. Such is no longer the case. By 1965, 80 per cent of the population was living in cities and towns; the remainder, including the 3 per cent who live on the collective farm settlements, were rural dwellers.

HOW THE NEW STATE CAME TO BE

At the outbreak of World War I in 1914, there were eighty-five thousand Jewish settlers in Turkish-ruled Palestine. Although the Turks were allies of Germany and enemies of Great Britain, the Jews of Palestine were wholeheartedly on the British side. A legion of Jews fought as part of the British army against their Turkish rulers. In 1917, British Foreign Secretary Lord Balfour issued a declaration of sympathy with Zionist aims. The Zionists hoped (and expected) that Arab and Jew would live peacefully side by side in a new Jewish state in Palestine. At first, Arab leaders were sympathetic with the Jewish cause. Agreements signed at the Paris Peace Conference at the end of the war divided most of Turkey's domains in Asia into independent Arab states. The exceptions were Anatolia, which remained Turkish, and Palestine, which was to be governed by Great Britain until its people should be ready to form their own government. The League of Nations Mandate (a word that means "command") recognized the Zionist cause as expressed in the Balfour Declaration. Filled with hope, Jews from war-torn Europe poured into Palestine. They bought more land, planted more trees, irrigated dry fields, and drained marshes. The once poor country began to prosper.

Meanwhile, a new war was on the way. Hitler, the dictator of Germany, was blaming everything that had gone wrong in his country on the Jews. His announced purposes were to make Germans the master race of the world, and to exterminate the Jews. To achieve his first aim, he invaded the lands on Germany's borders. Britain, France, the United States, and their allies went to war against him. By the time World War II ended in Hitler's defeat, six million Jews had been killed in ghettos, concentration camps, and prisons.

Zionists in Israel in 1921. (Zionist Archives and Library)

Names of concentration camps appear on the floor of the Tent of Remembrance in Jerusalem's Memorial Shrine, built in memory of the six million Jews killed during the Nazi period.

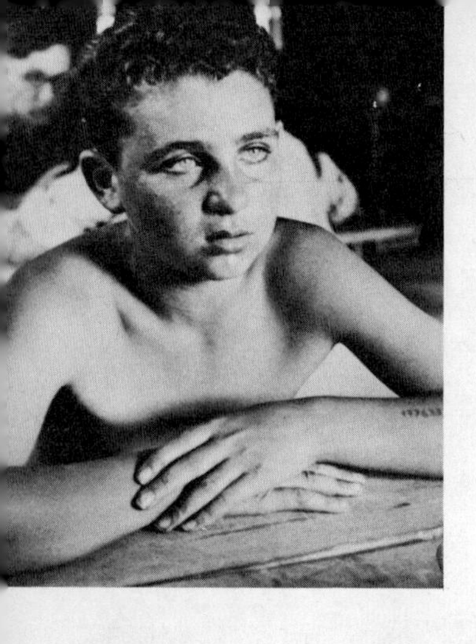

A young victim of a Nazi concentration camp, with his prisoner number tattooed on his arm. (Zionist Archives and Library)

The surviving Jews of Europe had been starved, beaten, and tortured. They had lost their homes and their families. They had suffered so much that they could never again feel safe in the countries where they had been born. Many would feel safe only among their own people in Palestine. Others who might have preferred a more comfortable life were kept out of the countries of their choice by immigration laws. The Arab landowners did not wish Jews to be admitted to Palestine either. They had seen how Jews brought with them disturbing Western ideas of higher wages, equal rights for women, and better education for all. Arab leaders stirred up the ignorant farmers in their lands with arguments based on religious hatred and their fear of those who were different from themselves.

The Jewish settlements were attacked and sabotaged. Since the British police did not protect them, the Jews of Palestine organized their own semi-secret defense force, the Haganah. There were bloody clashes. Using this conflict as an excuse, the British officials sharply limited the number of Jews permitted to enter Palestine. The Haganah brought them in anyway, by night, in leaky little ships that landed on lonely beaches. From there these immigrants were spirited away into hiding on the collective settlements. Some were caught and sent to detention camps. But the violence grew steadily worse. Britain brought the quarrel to the United Nations.

In November, 1947, the United Nations General Assembly approved a resolution to partition Palestine into two independent states: one Arab, the other Jewish. The Jews agreed. The Arab countries said publicly that they would use force to prevent the resolution from being carried out. Armed attacks on Jewish settlements by Arab bands within Palestine and from across the border mounted into full-scale war.

Six months later the Mandate ended, and the last British soldiers left the country. On the fifth of Iyar, according to the Jewish calendar — May 14, 1948 — the State of Israel declared its independence and was recognized by the United States.

A few hours later, the forces of Egypt, Jordan, Syria, Lebanon, and Iraq plus a contingent from Saudi Arabia, crossed into Israel in tanks and bombed the tiny nation from the air. That was how Israel's War of Independence, or War of Liberation, began — not very long ago. Many Israelis remember well how their settlements were machine-gunned; or how hungry they were during the siege of Jerusalem, or, in Tel Aviv, how they had to dodge behind hastily erected shelters to escape the fire from the mosque tower in nearby Jaffa.

Jews arriving in Palestine after World War II pass British officials. (United Press International)

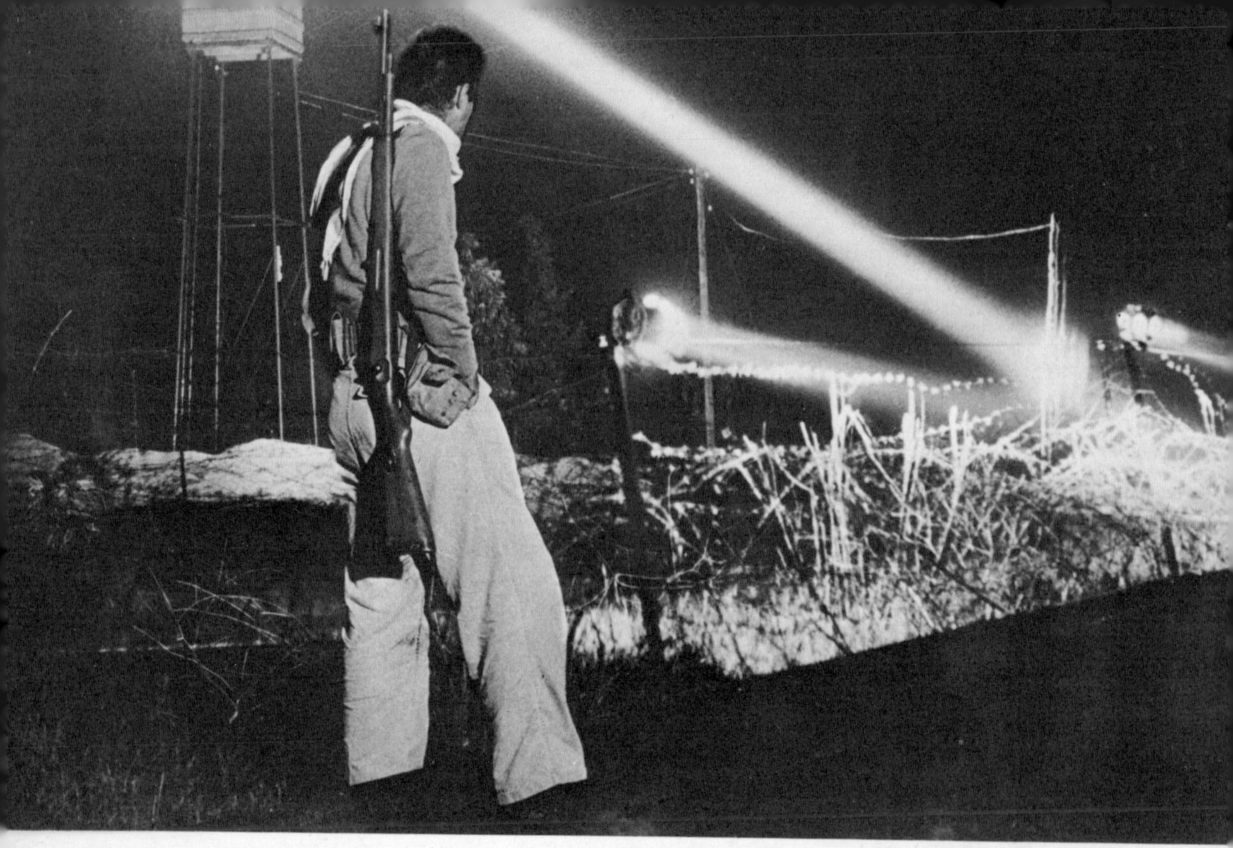

On night patrol in a Jewish settlement.

After seven months of war, the United Nations brought about a truce. The Arabs had been badly beaten by an Israeli force which was smaller and not as well supplied with arms. But the Israelis were fighting for their home. According to the armistice agreement signed by both sides, Israel kept the land beyond the partition lines, which had been taken in bitter fighting, but lost Old Jerusalem, where Jews had always lived, where the Temple had stood. Only one small part of the ancient city was to remain in Israeli hands: Mount Zion. On May 11, 1949, Israel became a member of the United Nations. Its flag — a blue Star of David and two blue stripes on a white ground — flies today at United Nations headquarters in New York.

The announcement of the establishment of the new state said, in part:

> The State of Israel will be open to the immigration of Jews from all the countries of their dispersion;
> will promote the development of the country for the benefit of all its inhabitants;
> will uphold the full social and political equality of all its citizens without distinction of religion, race or sex;
> will safeguard the Holy Places of all religions;
> and will loyally uphold the principles of the United Nations charter.

Israel's flag is hoisted at the old United Nations headquarters in Lake Success, New York, in May, 1949.

Newly arrived oriental Jews.

"THE INGATHERING OF THE EXILES"

One of the first laws passed by the new government was the Law of the Return, which recognized the right of Jews to live in Israel.

As soon as the British moved out, the newcomers streamed in. They spoke German, Polish, Rumanian, Arabic, French, English, and a dozen other languages, even Hindustani. Most were without money and with only enough possessions to make up a small bundle. Many were sick. Some were too old to work and some too young.

The first oriental Jews to come to Israel were from Yemen, a backward kingdom in the far-off southwestern corner of the Arabian peninsula, where Jews are said to have lived since biblical times. Yemenite Jews claim that their forefathers fashioned the metal doors for King Solomon's Temple. They are still good at making things such as jewelry, gardens, and the embroidered blouses that are favorites with both Israeli girls and tourists. The Yemenites are a small and lively people who, no matter what their age, will dance till dawn if given a chance. They had always taught their children to read the Torah, and their Hebrew is the pure language of Scripture. The Yemenites fitted quickly into their promised land.

For others it has not been so smooth. Many have come from Arab lands where the poor are illiterate and underprivileged, and where Jews were kept at a standard of living lower than that of the poorest Arab. There are Jews in Israel now who have lived in mountain caves or in the filthy slums of North African cities; Jews who cannot read or write, who had never slept in a bed, sat on a chair, brushed their teeth, or known modern plumbing conveniences, or doctors. Their families are large because it is an honor in Arab communities for a man to have as many children as possible even if he cannot feed them. No one has time to show these children books or explain anything to them. When they disobey, they expect to be beaten. Since the father is usually an unskilled laborer, the family remains poor. When the children learn new, modern ways of life in school, they often lose respect for their parents, which causes more trouble in the family.

An Israeli statesman once compared his country to a pressure cooker, which could rapidly turn out a well-mixed stew from a variety of ingredients. The city planners have come to realize that if too much pressure is applied, the pot may explode. Newcomers from oriental lands have habits so widely different from those of Europeans that no amount of pressure can make the two groups get along at close quarters. A housewife accustomed to preparing meals at a kitchen table can see no reason why the tenant of the flat overhead has to pound up her food on the floor.

Waiting for relatives to arrive at Haifa's port.

The Lachish area (of which you will hear more later) has found a way to avoid such quarrels. In one village, all the settlers are Rumanian; in the second, they may be Persian; in the third, Moroccan; in the fourth, Egyptian — and so on. Each family is surrounded by neighbors whose native language and customs it understands. The children of different villages meet at the rural primary schools, which are shared by five or six villages, or at the high school in the city of Kiryat Gat. Their elders get to know their fellow Israelis more slowly, at the farm-supply store in the town, or at the shopping center or community hall in Kiryat Gat.

Nevertheless, the strain between Jews of European, and Jews of oriental origin is a problem. The European community, which settled earlier, is richer and better educated, and holds down the majority of the white collar jobs. The orientals, who are on the way to becoming the largest segment of the population, resent what they consider to be discrimination. It is a problem that hopefully time and education can solve.

NON-JEWS IN ISRAEL

Village Arabs living in Palestine in May, 1948, when the British officials moved out, heard a broadcast from a neighboring Arab state advising them to leave home because the Jews were about to kill them. The broadcast said the Jews would be pushed into the sea shortly, and that the Arabs would then be able to return and add the Jews' land to their own. The Arabs who followed the advice lived thereafter in miserable refugee camps across the border in Jordan or in the Egyptian-controlled Gaza Strip. For the most part, their Arab brothers neither resettled nor employed them, and they are being supported by the United Nations. But the Arabs who remained peacefully at home are now citizens of

At the market in Acre one can see the minaret of the Great Mosque.

Israel, enjoying things that village Arabs never had before: free schooling, free medical care, electricity, and piped-in water.

City Arabs do the same kinds of work that city people do everywhere — carpentry, plumbing, factory and clerical work. Educated Arabs may be lawyers, teachers, businessmen, or architects.

In 1966, native Arabs made up 11 per cent of Israel's population of 2,500,000. An Arab citizen of Israel has voting rights like any other Israeli. He is represented in the legislature and in the labor unions. Arab villages are governed by their own local councils and have their own religious courts and judges. Arabic, the second official language of the country, appears on coins and stamps, and on many road signs. It is the teaching language in schools for Arab children.

The Negev Arabs are Bedouins who wander in the desert with their flocks just as their ancestors did centuries before. But even they are beginning to change.

Most Arabs are Muslims, who believe in the prophet Muhammad. Their holy book, the Koran, is based in part upon the Old Testament. Some of the Israeli Arabs are Christians who live mainly in Nazareth and its surrounding villages.

Altogether there are twenty-four different Christian sects represented in Israel. Walking the streets of Jerusalem, you might see a brown-robed Franciscan friar; or a nun in a starched white flyaway coif; a tall, dark Ethiopian monk; a Greek Orthodox priest whose long hair is pulled back in a chignon.

The Druzes live on Mount Carmel, in Galilee, and across the border in Syria and Lebanon. They are very secretive about their religion, but it is known to have been an offshoot of the Muslim faith many centuries ago. The Druzes identify their prophet Shu'ab with Jethro, the father-in-law of Moses. Though their language is Arabic, they were always persecuted by the Arabs and

A Bedouin girl on a donkey, the taxi of the Negev. (United Press International)

A Franciscan Brother at the ruins of a synagogue in Capernaum.

therefore fought on the side of the Jews in the War of Independence.

The Druzes are industrious farmers, excellent stonemasons and builders, and fine dancers. The village elders wear long black gowns and red caps wound about with white. The young men have adopted Western clothes, but the girls, as soon as they marry, put on the old costume of black or bright-colored gowns and graceful white head-scarves. The men enjoy more freedom in every way than the women, who remain shyly in the background, doing embroideries for their homes and weaving baskets for sale. The Druzes love color and use it well, in basketry and on their houses.

THE GOVERNMENT OF ISRAEL

Israel is a republic. The government consists of a legislature, a president, a prime minister, and a cabinet. Every Israeli citizen eighteen years of age or older may vote for the 120 members of the Knesset, the Hebrew name for the legislature. The Knesset chooses the president. His term lasts five years, but may be renewed once for five more years. The president formally appoints some of the other high officials; he approves treaties and signs laws that have been passed by the Knesset. After consulting with the Knesset, he appoints the prime minister from the party that holds the most seats in the Knesset. The prime minister chooses the members of his cabinet — the ministers of education, labor, housing, foreign affairs, and other branches of the administration. The cabinet can suggest laws to the Knesset, which in turn votes upon them. The prime minister and the cabinet carry them out.

The first president of Israel was Chaim Weizmann, chosen in

Opening of the new Knesset building.

David Ben-Gurion, the country's first Prime Minister, announces the birth of Israel on May 14, 1948. Behind him hangs a portrait of Theodor Herzl, founder of modern Zionism.

recognition of his accomplishments in the cause of Zionism. Because Dr. Weizmann was a scientist of international fame, it was possible for him to exert considerable influence in many parts of the world, particularly in England, where the Balfour Declaration was conceived.

The first prime minister was David Ben-Gurion. While still a young man, Ben-Gurion left his native Poland and came to Palestine as a pioneer. When "B.G." resigned from office some years ago, he retired to Sdeh Boker, a kibbutz in the Negev, where he had earlier established his home as an example to young Israelis.

Israel has twelve or more political parties. There are parties which specifically represent Arabs, while others represent Jewish religious groups. A cause of severe conflict is the widespread difference of opinion on how thoroughly the laws of the state should conform to the law of the Torah (as, for example, the rules relating to marriage, burial, preparation of food, observance of the Sabbath). The religious parties hope to see these laws incorporated into the constitution, while the majority of Israelis would prefer that such matters be left to individual choice. Israel has no written constitution as yet. From time to time the Knesset passes basic laws which will eventually be put together as the constitution of the state.

THE LANGUAGE OF ISRAEL

A stubborn, sickly little man named Elieser Ben-Yehuda arrived from Russia in 1881, determined to make the Jews of Palestine speak Hebrew. Since ancient times it had not been the language of daily life, but only of the synagogue, the prayers, and the holy books. Nonreligious literature was also written in Hebrew at times, particularly by the Jews of medieval Spain under Moorish rule. To Ben-Yehuda however goes the credit for reviving it in daily speech, through his teaching and his own example. He refused to utter a word in any other tongue, even at home with his family. The idea soon spread, and Ben-Yehuda spent the remainder of his life writing the first dictionary of modern Hebrew.

As more Jews came to Israel from different countries, a national language became a necessity. Eastern European Jews could understand one another by speaking Yiddish (also called "Jewish"), a mixture of Old German, Hebrew, and words from various languages. But Yiddish was unknown to the Jews of Iraq, North Africa, and other eastern countries — the so-called oriental Jews.

The official language of Israel is based on Old Testament Hebrew. Words for objects that did not exist in Old Testament times have been invented, such as *aviron,* for "airplane," from *avir,* the Hebrew word for "air." The Hebrew alphabet is called the *Alef-Bet,* and is an ancestor of our own. It lacks some of our letters, has others that we do not, and looks quite different from our own. Hebrew is read from right to left, whereas Western languages are read from left to right.

Israeli newcomers go to school to learn their own language, and it is not an easy one. The *ulpan* is a special course given to teach adults enough Hebrew in five months to hold down a job that requires the use of the language. Children born in Israel (called *sabras,* after the sweet, prickly native cactus fruit) speak Hebrew as naturally as you speak the language of your country. Hebrew is the language of schools and government officials, and, increasingly, the language most often heard on the street and in the home.

FROM PLAY SCHOOL TO COLLEGE

Jews have traditionally emphasized the role of education for their children. Even in the poorest communities in the Diaspora, most children were taught to read and write, and the scholar was held in respect. In the Arab countries, however, it has been impossible for all Jewish children to obtain an education.

So it is not surprising to find a similar emphasis on education in Israel. In 1965, there were over 700,000 young people attending schools and colleges. The money allotted to education was the largest – next to defense – in the government budget.

The children of early settlers have a big edge over children of newcomers. One recent way of making up the difference has been

Young boys in school, wearing yarmulkes, or skullcaps, on their heads.

to provide free play schools for youngsters whose parents cannot afford to pay a fee. Primary school is free for everyone, and every child from five to fourteen must attend. The state has not yet been able to offer a free high-school education to all, but there are many scholarships, particularly for children of immigrants.

Some of these children of newcomers live in children's villages till their fathers have found jobs and the family is well settled in their new home. These children's villages were originally built to take care of those who had lost their parents in Hitler's Europe. Fortunately there are few orphans now, and the village facilities are used as boarding schools, where pupils spend half the day studying, and the other half working on the village farm or learning a trade.

Everywhere you go in Israel, you see groups of boys and girls hiking, singing as they march. Others, packed into trucks, leave behind them the sounds of singing too. These groups of happy youngsters can be seen visiting museums, swarming over ruins, camping on the beach or in the desert. They may belong to the Scouts, or to one of a dozen other youth groups. Their favorite kind of party is a *kumsitz* (from the German, "come sit") round a campfire at night. Hour after hour they sit and sing, clapping

A scout group at a kumsitz, a party around a campfire.

hands in time to the tune, and not bothering much about the words, which seem to be mostly "la-la-la!" Or they form a circle to dance the *hora,* the national folk dance, with their arms on each other's shoulders, jumping and stamping.

Neither girls nor boys as a rule go to college until after they have completed their military service. So, as freshmen, they are usually at least twenty years old. Tuition fees are high, and it is common for the college student to hold down a full-time job while he is studying. Therefore he most likely takes far more than four years to finish his studies, and may be married, with children, by the time he receives his degree.

More than twenty thousand students currently attend four institutes of higher learning. Two were founded before Israel became

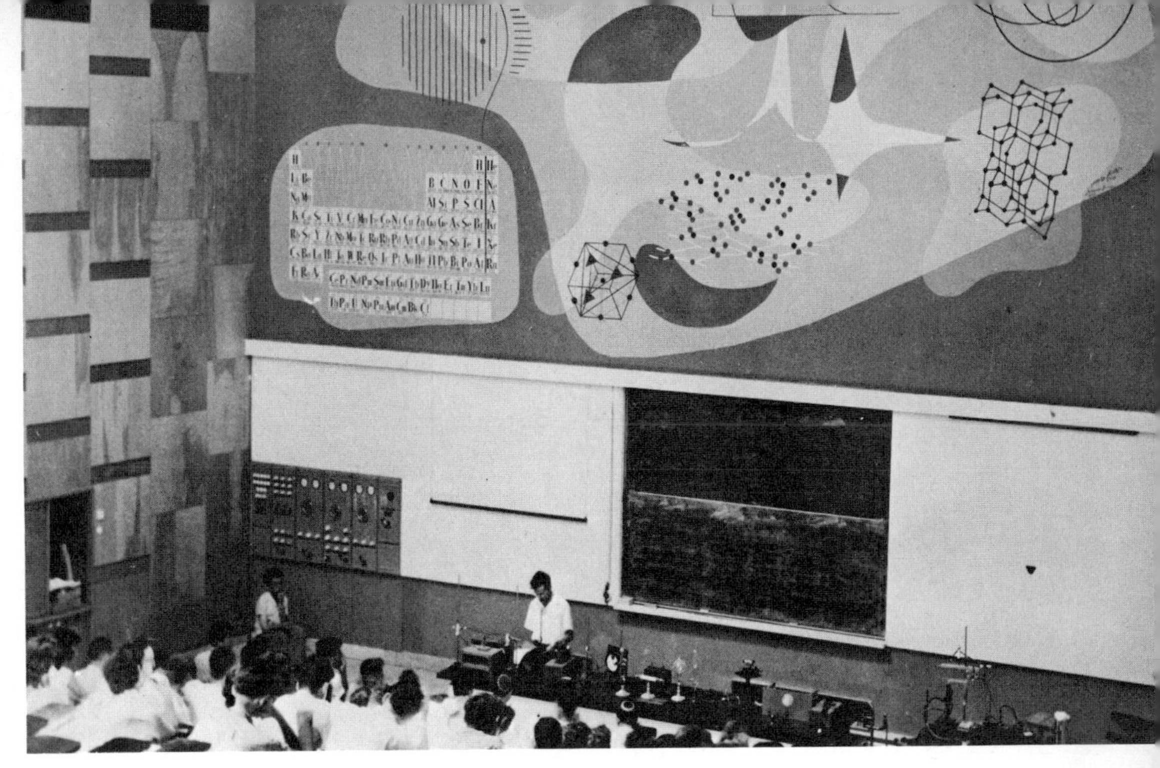

A chemistry lecture hall at the Hebrew University in Jerusalem.

a state: the Hebrew University at Jerusalem (1925) and the Technion at Haifa (1912), which trains engineers, technologists, architects, and scientists to work in Israel and abroad. Two more recently organized universities are Tel Aviv University, maintained by the city of that name, and Bar-Ilan University, a religious institution. There are also more than fifty teacher training colleges, almost two hundred *yeshivot* (talmudic colleges), and a number of Adult Education Centers. The Weizmann Institute of Science, named in honor of Chaim Weizmann, is a world-famous center for research and scientific study. Training in nuclear research, radiobiology and the like are carried on in association with the Israeli Atomic Energy Commission and Israel's nuclear reactor at Yavneh.

An Israeli girl serving as a field telephonist in the army.

THE ARMY OF ISRAEL

Except for a few deferments, all Israeli youngsters are called into the army, navy, or airforce at eighteen, the men to serve for a little more than two years; the women for about a year and a half. For many a young immigrant, the armed forces do the job of a school: no one finishes his period of service without having acquired Hebrew and the elements of a primary education if he has missed them.

In *Nahal* (Pioneering Fighting Youth) many young soldiers, after basic military training, spend one year doing civilian-type work in a border village which is so dangerous or so uncomfortable that few civilians are attracted to it. The girls do women's work: cooking, sewing, and light farm tasks — but they learn how to handle a gun as well as a boy does. The purpose of the Israel Defense Army is symbolized by its insignia: a sword entwined with an olive branch.

After his initial training, every Israeli within a certain age range is called up each year for a brief period of retraining. Thus a professional standing army of only 70,000 can, on short notice, become a civilian army of almost four times that size.

Jewish girls and Druze boys in Israel's army dance together in a Druze village.

DAYS OF CELEBRATION

YOM HA'ATZMAUT (Independence Day) is in May. (The exact date, as in all holidays, depends on the Jewish calendar, which is different from ours.) Like national holidays everywhere, it is marked by military parades before enormous excited crowds. "*Look* at our planes!" they cry, as the jets roar overhead.

Jewish religious holidays are also national holidays in Israel. In addition to the traditional type of observance, there are special customs that make one feel as if the events being celebrated happened only yesterday. Many holidays recall ancient customs.

ROSH HASHANAH, the Jewish New Year, comes in September or October. This and YOM KIPPUR, the Day of Atonement, nine days later, are the most important holidays of the religious year. In Israel, as elsewhere, they are observed by services in the synagogue. The unique aspect of Yom Kippur is the utter quiet; streets and roads are empty of all traffic.

SUCCOTH, or the Feast of Tabernacles, also comes in fall. It honors the booths (or tents) in which the Children of Israel dwelt on their journey from Egypt to the Promised Land. Traditionally Jewish families eat all of their meals during this week in outdoor arbors decorated with autumn fruits and foliage, particularly the *lulab* (palm branch) and *ethrog* (citron). This is the autumn harvest festival, once celebrated by water-pouring rites performed to bring on the rains for the crops. Israelis say, "It will rain after Succoth." And it often does.

SIMHATH TORAH, the Rejoicing of the Law, which comes next, marks the end of one annual cycle of Torah reading and the beginning of a new one. In the religious communities, the Scrolls of the Law are paraded to the accompaniment of mystic ceremonies, chanting, and music.

HANUKKAH, the Feast of Lights, is the midwinter festival. The holiday recalls the successful Maccabean revolt against the king of Syria. When the Temple was cleansed of its pagan desecration, one day's supply of holy oil miraculously burned for eight days. In Jewish homes one candle is lighted on the first night of Hanukkah, and one is added each night till eight are burning. In Israel, relay runners of Maccabi, the Israel Sports Association, light a torch at Mode'in, the town of the Maccabees, and run with it to kindle a big eight-branched candelabrum at Jerusalem.

TU BI-SHEVAT, the New Year of the Trees, in January or early February, is a day when children go out into the woods to plant new trees.

PURIM, in March, is a carnival holiday, a time for gaiety, costume parties, mummers, and dancing in the streets. The holiday honors Esther, the beautiful Jewish queen of Persia who saved her people from destruction at the hands of the wicked Haman.

PESACH (Passover), which comes in March or April, celebrates the escape from Egypt. In Israel as elsewhere, the holiday begins with a joyous family meal, the *seder*. There is extra meaning to readings and songs which remind Jews that they were slaves and are now free.

A Purim party in a kindergarten.

This young girl is celebrating Shavuoth, Feast of the First Fruits.

On LAG B'OMER, in May, bonfires are lit on hilltops because this day marks the miraculous end of a plague that afflicted the Jews during the last revolt against Rome. It is an occasion when Orthodox Jews (and others for the fun of it) make a pilgrimage to Merom, near Safad, to light candles at the tomb of a wonder-working medieval rabbi, to camp out, and sing and dance all night.

Toward the end of May comes the spring harvest festival, SHAVUOTH, Feast of the First Fruits, which in religious terms celebrates the receiving of the Law at Mount Sinai seven weeks after the Exodus from Egypt. On this day processions of people on foot and in farm trucks garlanded with flowers show their gratitude by bringing the produce of early summer to the Jewish National Fund. In ancient times these offerings of grain, cheeses, and chickens were brought to the Temple.

TISH 'A B'AV, usually in late July, commemorates the ninth day of the Hebrew month of Av, when the Temple was destroyed.

A Christian celebration at the Church of the Beatitude on the Sea of Galilee.

SHABBAT (Sabbath) has a holy significance in Israel far beyond the day of rest observed in other lands. From sundown on Friday to sundown Saturday, Israelis rest and mark the holiday in various ways: the religious, at the synagogue or at home; the nonreligious, at the beach, visiting friends, and generally enjoying the day off. On Friday night one and all greet each other with *Shabbat Shalom* — "a peaceful Sabbath to you."

Christians in Israel celebrate all their religious holidays: Good Friday, Easter, Christmas, Ascension Day, Pentecost, and others.

Muslims also celebrate their festivals: Ramadan and the birthday of Muhammad.

The great Druze celebration, once a year, is a pilgrimage to the tomb of the prophet Shu'ab, in the hills above Tiberias.

Planted fields in the Valley of Israel.

FOOD FOR THE TABLES OF ISRAEL

Before he can plant seeds in the neglected fields, the Israeli farmer must clear them of stones — a backbreaking job. If the seeds are to sprout, they must have water. Since it does not rain in this part of the world from May to October, he cannot depend upon rain; one third of all farmland has to be artificially watered. Most sources of water — springs, rivers, lakes — are in the north. Huge pipes now bring this water to the thirsty farms of the south, where they connect with a network of portable irrigation pipes running through the fields.

Occasionally these days a few drops do fall in summer. The trees have attracted rain; since the Jews came back to Palestine about 100,000 acres of trees have been planted. Israelis like to show visitors their new forests, many of them planted through gifts from overseas.

The grapevine and the olive tree, which grow well in dry stony soil, were good producers in ancient times. Century-old trees with gnarled, twisted limbs still produce olives for eating and for making olive oil. Wine, a popular drink in lands where there is little water, is made in Israel for domestic use and for export. Today, the Israeli prefers fruit juice (which he calls *mitz*) to wine. In addition to their use domestically, fresh oranges and grapefruit are exported.

The money they bring in is used to buy necessities, such as coffee, which are not grown in Israel.

Cucumbers, eggplant, and melons are other plants native to this dry climate. Israelis make a salad of cooked eggplant, or chopped cucumbers, tomatoes, and onions and eat it twice a day — for supper and breakfast — together with cheeses of different kinds, herrings, olives, and leben, a sour-milk product invented by the desert Arabs. The melons are delicious. In summer you will see great heaps of yellow sugar melons and green watermelons for sale along the highways. Each year new varieties of fruit and vegetables not native to the country are successfully introduced and grown in Israel. These include apples, bananas, plums, avocados, lettuce, string beans, peas, and asparagus.

The land now produces three-quarters of the food its people eat. There is a surplus of eggs and an abundance of turkey and chicken. Some meat is supplied by the few cattle ranches. Vast herds of sheep are raised for their milk which is used in making cheese. One kind of farm original with Israel is the fish farm, where carp are grown in artificial ponds. The carp provide a cheap source of protein and the basis for gefüllte fish, a traditional Jewish dish, which is eaten on Friday nights and on special occasions.

An Israeli cowboy with his cattle on one of the country's few ranches.

Israeli technicians help build a new hotel in Africa.

WESTERN TECHNOLOGY IN AN EASTERN LAND

Constantly being added to the lists of Israeli products are new items made for use in manufacturing and for export. All across the land you will see white-tufted plants — cotton for the textile mills. Galilee is green with tobacco, grown mostly by Arab farmers. Peanuts are a popular crop, for eating, oil, and peanut butter. Flowers are grown for home use and their bulbs for export. Peaches and strawberries, which ripen in the Negev in winter, fetch high prices in northern markets.

Israel's economic planners realized that their young nation could not subsist upon agriculture alone. It would have to develop its relatively few resources by the most efficient methods available. So every native product — cement, sand for making glass, minerals, chemicals, marble — is exploited to the utmost. Other items, such as Israeli fashions and industrial diamonds, owe their success to the application of skilled workmanship on imported materials.

In today's world, "being able to get there quickly" is of primary importance. Israel's national airline, El Al, started with two civilian planes in 1949. Now it has several jets and turboprops flying to major airports on four continents. All of its pilots are Israeli citizens, 90 per cent of whom serve in the Israeli air force.

These accomplishments make the small, poor, young country the one modern state in the Middle East. They are the result of intensive research and ingenuity applied to domestic resources and to the best materials imported from abroad. And now Israel has a new export item: its young, home-trained scientists and technologists who are transmitting their know-how to other small, poor young nations of the world.

THE NEGEV

In the Negev Desert it rains only 10 to 20 days in the entire year. Yet archeologists who have explored it know that remote parts of this dry land formerly supported a settled population. Seeing Avdat, an ancient city whose white ruins look down on parched earth for miles around, makes you ask: How did these people live? They did it by damming up the stream beds which are dry during the summer, so that in winter the dams would block floodwaters that would otherwise have been lost by running off into the Dead Sea, or sinking into the ground. Israeli engineers are experimenting with similar methods to construct reservoirs of water in the desert.

There are a few hidden springs along the old camel caravan routes, and water prospectors are constantly drilling for more. Unfortunately, the water they find is often too salty to be useful. Scientists are seeking ways to change salt water into fresh. The methods developed up to now have been too expensive to be practical. It is hoped that nuclear power, generated by Israel's atomic reactor, will lower the cost.

Most of the water supply for the south is piped in from the north. For several years the rolling hills of the upper Negev, above Beersheba, have been covered with golden grain. Farther south, new settlements and even cities are made possible by the opening of the National Water Carrier, a conduit which, despite Arab

Ein Avdat — a hidden pool in the desert.

threats to destroy it, carries water from the Sea of Galilee to the desert. It runs through tunnels, canals, and in pressurized pipes over whole mountain ranges.

Beersheba, the capital of the Negev, has always had water; its name means "Seven Wells." Under the Turks it was a small, dusty outpost in a desolate, sparsely populated wilderness. Only a few years ago, it was a town with the adventurous atmosphere of the American West in early days. Its frontiersmen were young, tough Israelis, and the Arabs were to them what the Indians were to the American settlers.

Beersheba has grown so rapidly that in 1965, almost a hundred industries were located there, supporting a population of seventy thousand. Many more newcomers – including the twenty-five hundred babies born annually – are expected. Thousands of tourists pass through the new city, sometimes staying at a luxury hotel, which is modeled after one in the California desert.

Yet Beersheba is still a frontier town. A few miles out you will see only two kinds of human habitation in the large open spaces: an occasional new kibbutz, or a Bedouin encampment of a few lonely black tents with camels, goats, dogs, and horses roaming about. Early every Thursday, the Negev Bedouins ride or walk or hitchhike to the camel market at Beersheba, where they squat, exchange news, and sell their animals and the rolls of goat-hair tent cloth woven by their women. Afterward they stroll the streets of Beersheba and finish the week's shopping.

The Bedouin way of life is hard, with little to eat and much sickness. Yet these wanderers have been reluctant to give it up. The Bedouin still prefers his camel to a motorcycle. Some of the tribes have at last been persuaded to settle in villages and cultivate the soil with tractors and chemical fertilizers, and to send their sick to the hospital at Beersheba, and their children to school.

Parts of the southern Negev can never be farmed. This is a true desert of rocks and mountains carved by wind and weather into the shape of monsters and ruined castles. There are rich minerals and chemicals here which science and modern business can put to use. A seven-mile long hole in the ground, the Big Crater, produces clay for porcelain tiles, bathtubs, decorative pottery, and ordinary dishes. The salts of the Dead Sea are refined into ingredients for fertilizers, washing detergents, and a dozen other necessities. Some fuel oil has been found, as well as a good deal of natural gas which can be used for cooking and heating, as well as firing machinery. At Timna, near Elath, copper is being mined for the first time since King Solomon's day.

The Bedouin still prefers his camel.

The Timna copper works in the Negev.

The site of King Solomon's port, Ezion-geber, is in Jordan, a few miles across the Gulf of Aqaba from the new Israeli port of Elath. In the days of King Solomon ships sailed to mysterious Ophir, and brought back "gold and silver, ivory, and apes, and peacocks." Today ships sail from Elath with copper, chemicals, refrigerators, and farm products for ports in Africa and the Far East. They return with radios and cameras from Japan; shoe leather and wool from East Africa. A long, recently completed road, which Israelis call their dry canal, runs from the port of Elath to the port of Ashdod; from the Red Sea (an arm of the Indian Ocean) on the east, to the Mediterranean Sea (an arm of the Atlantic) on the west.

In summer the temperature at Elath averages 104 degrees. Water is so scarce that some of it *must* be supplied by desalinated sea-water, expensive though it is. One would think this a dangerous and uncomfortable place to live, with Jordan on the east, the Sinai Desert on the west, and Saudi Arabia on the south. Yet the citizens of Israel's southern-most town say they wouldn't live anywhere else. "We are the last pioneers!" they boast.

You can fly to Elath from Tel Aviv in an hour, or drive down in less than a day. You can swim in the Red Sea, which is cobalt blue. You can put on a mask and snorkel and float over coral gardens where the fish are bright as butterflies. You can camp out on the beach or in the desert hills behind the town. Or stay in an air-conditioned hotel. For a winter vacation, Elath is hard to beat. And now "development" has come to this little town, too. The network of artificial lagoons and canals, hotels, and other attractions now being planned will transform Elath into a resort where sailing, water-skiing, canoeing, and fishing can be enjoyed. Its pioneer flavor is doomed.

Ships docked at Elath.

ANCIENT CITIES AND BRAND-NEW ONES

There is always a reason why people settle in a particular place. Jerusalem was a mountain stronghold, defended by the steepness of its approaches. Beersheba was an oasis. Megiddo and Hazor stood at the crossroads of ancient trade routes.

Megiddo and Hazor are dead cities marked by *tells*. A tell is a hill formed over the ages by a succession of settlements built one over the other, each one upon the ruins of an earlier one. Israel has hundreds of such tells, some partly explored, others awaiting the spade of the archeologist.

New cities in Israel, like the old ones, develop for good reasons, and not because a government expert closes his eyes, puts a finger on a map at random, and says, "Let's build it here." One town may be designed to be the center of a farming district; another as a manufacturing center that must be close to the source of raw materials. The many acres of state-owned land in Israel make it possible to plan in advance not only where a new town will be, but what industries will be developed to make a living for its population, how many housing units it will begin with, where the synagogue and school will be, and so on.

One day there is a hillside, a sand dune, or a desert with nothing on it as far as the eye can see. The next day the place swarms with architects and engineers who draw up plans for the new city, and with workmen who will carry out the plans. The town goes up like a child's toy-town built of blocks. Then one day it is finished. New tenants arrive and move into the empty flats. At first the town looks barren and ugly. Dust swirls through unpaved streets in which the children play. But in a short while – perhaps no more than a year – there is a playground for the children, and a bright new shopping center for the housewives. There are flowers in the yards, and

A new city in the Negev (above) and the view from it (below).

after a longer time, trees and grass. Plants grow marvelously fast in the sun and soil of Israel. All they need is water.

Tell ed-Duweir, in central Israel, has been identified as Lachish, a fortress city that once rose in the midst of that flat dry land. It had an elaborate but unfinished water system. From the day when the last settlement on the tell vanished, the area had been abandoned by man. It lacked water for probably two thousand years.

Yet it is good, fertile farmland. By piping in water from the springs of the Yarkon River, which would otherwise have run uselessly into the sea at Tel Aviv, the Lachish district was opened to farming. Among the products raised there are cotton, sugar beets, peanuts, and vegetables. The area supports fifty-six villages and a central town, Kiryat Gat. The cotton gin, the sugar refinery, the peanut-butter and peanut-oil factory, and the packing plants are located in Kiryat Gat; so is the high school for the district, the seat of the local government, the hall for movies and concerts, and the big shopping center. Teachers, doctors, social workers, and other professionals who serve the villages live in "the big city" too.

MAN-MADE SEAPORT

Haifa Bay is the only real indentation in Israel's long Mediterranean coastline. Up to 1965, it was the only harbor on the west that could take a modern liner or oceangoing freighter. Every item and passenger going to and from the country had to pass through that crowded port.

The deepwater harbor of Ashdod had been envisioned since the foundation of the state. After an active planning stage of three years, and four years of building, the dream was finally realized. First to go up on the flat yellow beach was the city: long rows of apartment houses, shops, factories. By 1966, thirty thousand peo-

Building the harbor at Ashdod.

ple were living there, many of them French-speaking newcomers from France's former possessions in North Africa.

Only a few years ago the harbor was open sea. About one square mile has been walled in for a deepwater anchorage to accommodate thirty-two ships at one time. Boulders weighing up to twelve tons apiece were brought overland from quarries — 2½ million tons of rock altogether. The outer face of each breakwater is protected by tetrapods, four-legged concrete constructions, which interlock and dig themselves into the sand. These bear the brunt of the strongest waves.

Inside the harbor, along the shore, are piers for berthing ships, automatic cranes for hoisting cargo into and out of their holds, tanks of ships' fuel, warehouses, and machine shops. A new red and white lighthouse on a nearby dune flashes its welcoming beacon fifteen nautical miles out to sea.

No passenger boats dock in Ashdod. The present purpose of the port is to eliminate the cost of transporting freight by truck and railroad to Haifa, and to relieve the overcrowding there. From now on Ashdod will supply the factories of the south with their raw materials from abroad, and ship out their finished goods, along with chemicals from the Dead Sea, and citrus fruit from newly planted southern groves. The first vessel to arrive at Ashdod harbor was a Swedish freighter with sugar from Poland. The first one to go out carried oranges and grapefruit to England.

Tucked away near the railroad siding, where you would never notice it unless you were told, is little Tell Mor, the grass-covered remains of the port of ancient Ashdod, where ships took shelter thirty-five hundred years ago at the mouth of a little stream now diverted and dry.

Ancient Ashdod itself, one of the largest cities of Canaan, was located further inland. Its tell is presently being excavated by a joint Israeli-American team that hopes to uncover the secret of the ancient Philistines. This mysterious people, who probably came from the islands of the Aegean, have disappeared completely—but have left their name, Pulasti, to Palestine.

THE MANY FACES OF MOUNT CARMEL

The thickly clustered white buildings of Haifa, second largest city in Israel, climb steeply from the busy harbor district to the luxurious homes on the top of Mount Carmel. The Carmelit, a mile-long subway, connects what Haifa residents call "downstairs" with "upstairs."

Carmel is not a single mountain but a mountain range: a series of ridges and plateaus separated by small valleys. It is a region of numerous caves that were long inhabited by man. About 200,000 years ago, the caves were home for a squat, hairy race. The climate was hot and rainy; the swamps below the caves were populated by rhinoceroses, hippopotamuses, and elephants. The cavemen defended themselves and hunted food with roughly chipped flint weapons. The skulls and skeletons and the weapons of these early men have been excavated from the cave floors. About 100,000 years ago Carmel man appeared. He was apparently a mixture of the older type (Neanderthal man) and a more recent one that more closely resembled modern man (*Homo sapiens,* "thinking man").

Thousands of years later, in the time of the Old Testament, the caves of Carmel were still in use. In one of them (on the site of modern Haifa) the Hebrew prophet Elijah hid from the wrath of Ahab, king of Israel, whom he had denounced. The same Elijah is Saint Elias to the Carmelite monks, whose monastery stands high on a spur of the mountain above the cave. On another ridge of the Carmel is the beautiful new campus of the Technion. On the summit is a skyscraper hotel.

The city of Haifa climbs upward from the bay.

The mountain is what gives the city of Haifa its extraordinary view. Almost every house looks out over the great blue sweep of the bay, and down upon the harbor. The sea and the harbor are more important to Haifa than the mountain. The opening of the port at Ashdod has not diminished the noise and bustle on Haifa's docks. Derricks whine and cargo trucks scuttle about, loading and unloading the ships alongside. Newcomers, dazed or joyful, crowd the immigration shed. Tourists come down the gangplanks of cruise ships, astonished to find that the brawny porters and the customs officials in their crisp khaki uniforms are all Jews.

Haifa is the base for the navy, and for Israel's merchant fleet, which has grown from its founding in 1948 to about a hundred vessels. The men who command these ships got their first training in the small battered tubs that brought in the illegal immigrants during the British Mandate. In ancient days, Jews were not known as sailors. Like much else, this too has changed. Any day of the week you will see white sails on the horizon off Haifa. They are the fishing fleet, or racing sloops out of the Carmel Yacht Club, or the training boats of the Nautical Academy at Acre across the bay.

Haifa's industrial suburbs, factories, and homes of the workers, stretch northward from the outskirts of the city. If you drive around the bay to visit the Crusader remains at Acre and the mosque and quaint streets, you pass a cement factory; an automobile plant that makes the Susita ("little horse") sports car; the oil refinery, looking like two giant milk bottles; chemical plants that smell as bad as those on the Jersey flats; and Steel City, Israel's Pittsburgh.

Since Haifa is so large an industrial city, it is not surprising that the first united federation of Jewish workers, Histadrut, was formed there in 1920. This is a labor organization unlike any other: it is both a union of workingmen and a company in which all its mem-

The old city of Haifa.

Cement works near Haifa.

bers hold shares. Some Israelis think Histadrut is too powerful. It owns many of the factories and shops, the biggest building and public works company, a cooperative chain which sells farm products, a book publishing house, and three newspapers. It provides its members with insurance, doctors, dental clinics, rest homes, and folk dance and art groups. It plays an enormous part in politics.

From laying the cornerstone (above) to the modern city of Tel Aviv (below).

TEL AVIV — METROPOLIS ON THE BEACH

Tel Aviv was not planned; it just grew. About sixty years ago, the Jews who lived in the dark, cramped little houses of Arab Jaffa, built a European-style quarter on the sands to the north. Their new settlement grew larger and larger until it finally became a city. The old Arab town is the smallest part of this municipality known as Tel Aviv-Jaffa. Today Tel Aviv, with a population of almost 400,000, not including its suburbs, is the biggest, noisiest city in Israel.

A few Arabs and many oriental Jews still live in the old town in stone houses with vaulted ceilings, lovely ironwork, and (till recently) no plumbing. Since the port of Ashdod was opened, ships no longer put into Jaffa's little harbor from which the Bible tells us Jonah sailed on that unfortunate voyage when he was swallowed by a whale. Now there is a municipal park along the sea, and houses converted into artists' studios and nightclubs.

Even in winter the sea air keeps Tel Aviv warm. So the city is geared to outdoor living all year round. Men go to work in shorts and shirts open at the neck; women in sundresses. Every apartment has a balcony to serve as a family living room, drying yard, and a place from which to watch the street below and gossip with the neighbors. Every block has its sidewalk café where people sit for hours over coffee, soda, and ice cream, reading newspapers in many languages.

On early summer mornings you see people on their way to the big open-air swimming pool, with bathing suits under their robes and towels over their arms. They are off for a morning swim before going to work. The sea is no more than a short walk from most of Tel Aviv's homes. On Saturday, the beaches are so crowded that it is hard to find a few feet of sand on which to sit, or an empty chair among the thousands for rent. Families camp out for the day in bright-colored folding tents, with lunch baskets, playpens for the babies, and transistor radios. The lifeguard blows his shrill whistle and scolds the swimmers who venture far out, for this is a treacherous sea. Surfboats, guided by long double paddles, are shooting the waves. A favorite beach game, played with a small rubber ball and ping-pong rackets, goes on fast and furiously in dozens of places.

All up and down the coast there are beaches where these scenes are repeated. If you prefer quiet, you can find it, with difficulty, at a few beaches (usually owned by kibbutzim) where you can be alone, except for sandpipers and crabs.

There is no solitude to be found on Tel Aviv's overcrowded beaches.

Football — not the American game, but soccer — is the most popular spectator sport. Like all sports in Israel, it is played only by amateurs. The largest sports arena is at Ramat Gan, a suburb of Tel Aviv; it seats sixty thousand. When a National League or a championship soccer game is on, the excitement in Israel equals that in the United States during the World Series.

Tel Aviv has every sort of shop including many bookstores crammed with paperbacks, and American-style supermarkets. For amusement, you can go to a film made in Israel, or any number of foreign films; to a concert of the Israel Philharmonic, to the theater for a play by Shakespeare, or a Broadway hit translated into Hebrew, or the latest work of an Israeli playwright. Or you can sit at a café, or walk along the street, just watching other people.

Those who love Tel Aviv will admit that it is overcrowded, dirty, and noisy. But, they say, "It is so *alive*!"

JERUSALEM THE GOLDEN

You always go up to reach Jerusalem, for it is on a mountain, twenty-five hundred feet above sea level. In spite of being in a hot part of the world, Jerusalem and nearby Bethlehem do occasionally in winter have snow such as you see on Christmas cards.

The road to Jerusalem winds through a narrow pass between hills that are carved into very old vine terraces, and tufted with very old olive trees. Suddenly you come over the last rise and you are in New Jerusalem. Spread out before you are the government buildings and the Hebrew University with its football stadium. In the east are the church spires and cypresses on the Mount of Olives and the battlements of the Old City.

It is not only the road that goes "up." The devout of three religions believe that a man's soul is closer to heaven in Jerusalem

Both the old and the new can be found in Jerusalem.

than in any other place. It was there that King Solomon built the first Temple beside the Rock Moriah with its bronze altar for the people's offerings. Muslims say that their prophet Muhammad mounted a horse and sprang to Paradise from that same spot, and they have enclosed it in an elegant mosque, the Dome of the Rock. The Church of the Holy Sepulchre, enshrining the burial place of Jesus, is close by. Nothing remains of Solomon's Temple. Of the Temple built by Herod, all that is left is the western wall: the Wailing Wall, as it is known, is where Jewish pilgrims came for centuries to weep and to pray for Israel's restoration.

Israel is restored, but Old Jerusalem was lost to the Jews for nineteen years, for it was on the Jordan side of the line set by the armistice agreement of 1948. With its encircling walls and towers, Old Jerusalem looks like an enchanted, storybook city. And it *is* an enchanted city. It has been knocked down, burned with fire, strewn with salt – and it has risen again and again. At least four thousand years old, it is one of the oldest cities in the world in which people still live. It was old when King David chose it as his capital. The leaders of the new state chose Jerusalem too in preference to Tel Aviv. Israel, they said, could have no other spot as a capital. If not the Old City, then the New.

The streets of New Jerusalem, which led to gates of the Old City, ended in barbed wire, tank traps, and signs warning strangers of the danger of crossing the frontier into Jordan. The people who lived in those streets did not need to be warned. Gunfire has pockmarked their houses. And the armed sentries of the Arab Legion patrolling the battlements of the old walls, could not be overlooked.

Mount Zion, the part of the Old City which was always within Israel's borders, is a place of pilgrimage for both Christian and Jew. David's tomb is there, and above it is the room where Jesus and the disciples are believed to have celebrated the Last Supper, on

The walls of Old Jerusalem.

Passover Eve. The Dormitian Monastery and Church of the Benedictine Fathers stand in the garden where Mary, mother of Jesus, is said to have "fallen asleep."

Year by year, more new buildings spread out over the hills of New Jerusalem. The buildings are constructed of gold colored stone that has been taken out of the very ground on which they stand. Two recent buildings face one another across a wide paved thoroughfare: the new Knesset and the Israel Museum. In the archeological wing of the museum you can learn the history of the country through the objects (weapons, pots, ornaments, images of gods, parts of buildings) that have been dug up from its soil. The exhibits range from Jordan Valley pebble tools (the oldest kind of tool) through all the civilizations and invading forces that have left their traces in the land: Canaanite, Israelite, Philistine, Assyrian, Greek, Roman, and Crusader.

The Shrine of the Book houses history in ancient manuscripts: the scrolls found in caves near the Dead Sea and at Masada. Among them are the oldest Old Testament writings so far discovered.

The New City, built entirely by Jews, has some neighborhoods that are not very new. More than a hundred years ago, so many Jews returned to Jerusalem that they spilled over into sections beyond the walls of the old town. Mea She'arim (the Hundred Gates), walled like a ghetto for protection, was built in 1874. It is the stronghold of East European Jews who keep to the strict letter of the Law, and dress as their grandfathers did a century ago. The boys wear flat black hats, corkscrew curls over each ear, knee pants and thick black stockings even in midsummer.

You will find in Jerusalem every kind of Jew from every part of the world. On Saturday nights, Zion Square swarms with people of every color, in every costume from oriental pantaloons to the khaki uniforms of soldier boys and girls. Sweethearts walk hand in

Mount Zion, a holy place for Christians and Jews.

The Israel Museum in Jerusalem, opened in 1965.

hand. Fathers carry their small sons on their shoulders. Mothers push babies in their carriages. It is the end of the Sabbath day of rest, and time for fun. The movie theaters open. The kiosks do a brisk business in dried sunflower seeds, corn on the cob, soda pop, and *felafel,* the Israeli version of hamburger, made of ground chick-peas.

No one looks particularly poor, and no one particularly rich. The sabras may swagger a bit. "It is the free air of Israel that makes them so sturdy and strong," the older people say. "We have our own country again. And no one will take it from us."

These feelings echo the words of a Psalm, written during the Jewish exile in Babylon: "If I forget thee, O Jerusalem, let my right hand forget her cunning."

LAND WITHOUT PEACE

Despite the armistice agreements of 1948 and 1949, the Arab nations refused not only to sign peace treaties with Israel, but even refused to admit that there *was* a State of Israel. Trained Arab guerrillas were frequently sent across the borders to plant mines, and fired on farmers and innocent bus passengers, destroying whatever was within reach. Israel retaliated with punishing raids.

In 1956, to end terrorism stemming mainly from Egypt (officially the United Arab Republic), Israeli, French, and British troops captured bases in the Sinai Desert and fortifications blocking Israel's only entrance to the Red Sea. The victorious campaign was halted by a United Nations cease-fire resolution. In exchange for a guarantee of free passage to and from the Gulf of Aqaba, Israel agreed to withdraw her troops. The United Nations Emergency force (UNEF) was stationed on the Egyptian side of the border. While Israel said again and again that she wanted only

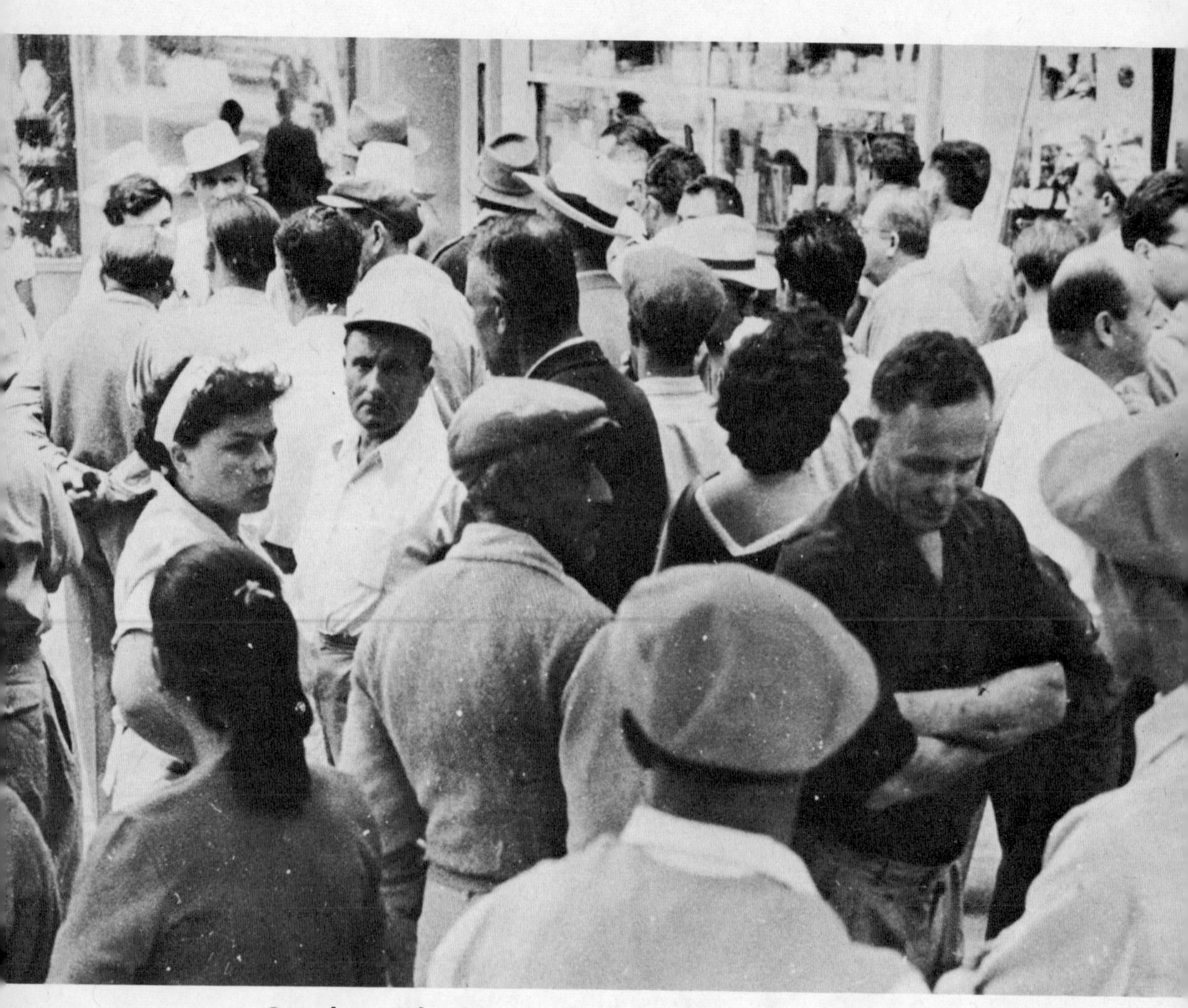

Crowds on Tel Aviv streets listen to war news in 1956. (United Press International)

peace, the Arab states publicly threatened to avenge their defeats by "another round."

This round became increasingly probable as more and more arms shipments arrived in the Middle East from abroad. The Soviet Union sent a billion and a half dollars' worth of submarines, jet aircraft, and the newest tanks and missiles to the Egyptian President Gamal Abdel Nasser. An additional billion dollars' worth of Soviet arms went to other Arab nations. The United States, which sold arms to Israel, helped Egypt with money, advice, and food.

Children emerging from an underground shelter after a clash between Israel and Syria. (United Press International)

After Egypt signed a mutual defense pact with Syria in November, 1966, terrorism increased, and Israeli settlements along the Syrian border were continually bombarded. Again Israel answered with a massive raid. There were skirmishes with tanks and in the air. On May 18, 1967, Syria's ally, Egypt, demanded the withdrawal of the United Nations peace-keeping force. President Nasser then moved up an army, recruited mostly from Palestinian refugees of 1948, to Israel's borders in Sinai and the Gaza Strip. Nasser then announced a new blockade of the Gulf of Aqaba. Israel declared that this was an act of war. Egypt's representative at the hastily summoned meeting of the United Nations Security Council stated that war had never ceased to exist in the Middle East. And in Arab cities everywhere, mobs screamed that they would wipe Israel's Jews off the earth.

The population of the Arab world is fifty times greater than that of Israel. Twelve Arab nations voiced support for Nasser's action. The combined armies of those directly involved (Egypt, Jordan, Syria, Lebanon, Iraq, Saudi Arabia) numbered almost six hundred and fifty-thousand soldiers, armored with more than three times as many tanks as Israel, and with almost three times as many planes – all of the latest Russian design.

General Moshe Dayan, who had commanded the successful 1956 Sinai campaign, was appointed Israel's Minister of Defense. As quietly as possible, the little country began to call its civilian reserves into the army. The major world powers urged all concerned parties to be patient. The Israelis obeyed. The Arabs threatened war. The United Nations took no action. At Gaza there were clashes and casualties. Early on the morning of June 5, in response to shelling by the Jordanians and Syrians, the Israeli Air Force swooped down upon twenty-five Arab airfields, wrecked their runways, and destroyed more than three hundred Egyptian aircraft

Israeli soldiers crossing the desert during the six-day war of 1967.

(mostly on the ground), which included long-range bombers designed to blot out Israeli cities. Then Israel's tanks moved south into the Sinai Desert.

In New Jerusalem, children, mothers, and grandparents camped in shelters for thirty hours while Jordan launched an attack from Old Jerusalem. All men of military age had gone off to fight — no one knew where. For days children had been helping to fill sandbags, dig trenches, and do grown-ups' jobs, such as delivering the

Civilians, both young and old, digging trenches during the 1967 conflict.

Jewish soldiers praying at the Wailing Wall in Old Jerusalem after the Israeli occupation of the city in 1967.

Arabs and Jews walk the streets of Old Jerusalem after the war.

mail. Taxicabs, buses, private cars, and trucks had been mobilized; even ice-cream trucks, camouflaged with mud, were used to deliver food to the army.

Israelis were fighting for their homes and for their country's existence. In three days they had taken the Gaza Strip; all of Sinai, with the Arab gun positions that blockaded the Gulf; and Jordan's territory west of the Jordan River (the section that had been part of Palestine until 1948). In taking Old Jerusalem, many Israelis lost their lives. For, to prevent damage to the holy places, the Israeli army employed only small arms instead of aerial bombing or long-distance shelling. On the fourth day of the war, Israel stormed the heavy fortifications and deep bunkers on the Syrian heights, from which destruction had been pouring down upon the villages below them. On the sixth day (June 10), Syria became the last of the Arab states to accept the United Nations resolution for a cease-fire.

Jerusalem was reunited. Barriers, tank traps, and barbed wire were cleared away. Now Jews from the New City and Arabs from the Old City freely intermingled. At last Jews could pray at the Wailing Wall, and Israeli Arabs could worship in the famous mosques of the Old City. There was, however, little celebration: too many people on both sides had been killed or crippled in this unnecessary war. In Jerusalem the Golden, for the first time in nineteen years, Arab and Jew said *Shalom* to one another, the Hebrew greeting that means "Peace." But permanent peace may not come to the troubled Middle East for a long time.

INDEX